THE LANGUAGE OF COMPUTERS

John Prenis

Star

A STAR BOOK
published by
the Paperback Division of
W. H. ALLEN & Co. Ltd

A Star Book
Published in 1981
by the Paperback Division of
W. H. Allen & Co. Ltd
A Howard and Wyndham Company
44 Hill Street, London W1X 8LB

First published in the United States by
Running Press 1977 as the Running Press Glossary of
Computer Terms.

Printed in Great Britain by
The Anchor Press Ltd, Tiptree, Essex

ISBN 0 352 30896 6

Preface

Computers are playing an increasingly large part in our lives. After some initial fears, we have learned to accept them, but still we do not feel comfortable with them. To most of us the computer is a faceless, impersonal genie that can produce without warning either technological wonders or foul-ups of monumental stupidity.

Our unease is due largely to our ignorance of computers. We feel that we are somehow being taken advantage of, a feeling that is too often true. Almost any mistake is excused if a computer can be blamed for it. Modern miracle products that have nothing to do with computers are labeled "computer this" or "computer that." And we know too little about them to protest when some badly thought-out feature of a computer system subjects us to indignity or inconvenience.

Unfortunately, the layman who tries to learn more about computers quickly runs into a problem. A language full of esoteric and colorful terms has grown up around computers. Slang, technical terms, and phrases coined by manufacturers all contribute to computer jargon. To the professional, it is a natural medium for expressing ideas; but to the layman, it is a puzzle.

The ultimate comment on this situation is a computer program that selects phrases and "buzz-words" at random and fits them together to make arbitrary sentences. The program will produce as many pages of this "computerese" as you want. The reader has the baffling feeling that what he is reading almost makes sense, but that the meaning is somehow eluding him.

Understanding what computers are all about does not require more than ordinary intelligence. But being able to speak the language is a great help. I have tried to make sure that all terms used are defined. If a technical term is used to define a more advanced term, the simpler term will be found elsewhere with its own definition. Where a term has more than one form, I have tried to define it under its most esoteric-looking form. Acronyms, for instance, are defined under their condensed rather than their spelled-out forms. Lest the reader be daunted, I should point out that it is quite possible to work with computers without knowing the vast majority of these terms. It is my hope that this book will help the reader to read books about computers, chat with computer people, or ask intelligent questions of computer salesmen. It is time that the computer became a tool rather than a mystery.

—*John Prenis*

About the Author

John Prenis had his first encounter with computers at the age of 12 during a summer workshop at the Franklin Institute in Philadelphia. Since then a devotee of electronics and computer science, he has studied computer programming at the University of Pennsylvania and has worked for General Electric in Advanced Development Engineering. Mr. Prenis, who has written and edited books on geodesic domes, herbs, and alternative energy sources, is presently at work building his own computer.

NOTE: *Italics* are used to indicate that a term in a definition is defined elsewhere in the glossary.

*[asterisk]. Because most printing mechanisms lack a times sign, computer languages often use an asterisk to indicate multiplication. A times B comes out as "A * B."

**[double asterisk]. Because most printers cannot handle superscripts, computer languages often use a double asterisk to indicate raising to a power. X to the Yth power or X^y comes out as "X ** Y."

ƀ[slashed "b"]. A lower case "b" with a slash through it is frequently used to indicate a blank.

Ø[slashed "O" or zero]. To prevent confusion between the letter "O" and zero, many program languages put a slash through one or the other. FØRTRAN slashes the letter "O," but BASIC slashes the zero.

↑[upward-pointing arrow]. Some languages use an upward-pointing arrow to indicate exponentiation. X^y comes out as X↑Y.

Abend. Short for "abnormal end," meaning that a program has been terminated by the computer for some reason.

Absolute addressing. An addressing mode in which the instruction contains or precedes the actual address of the memory location to which it refers.

Accumulator. Accumulator is another name for a *register*. The name seems to come from one of its functions: adding up sub-totals and holding the results. Some computers have only one general purpose register, which is then called the accumulator, the other registers being only temporary storage locations.

ACM. This abbreviation stands for the Association for Computing Machinery, the major professional society for computer people.

A/D converter. This device converts *analog* information to *digital* form.

Address. Each location in a computer memory is numbered consecutively. The number is referred to as the location's address.

Address register. A register in the CPU that contains the address of the *operand* currently in use.

Addressing modes. There are many ways in which a computer instruction can refer to a memory address. Some of the addressing modes are *absolute, direct, indirect, relative, indexed,* and *implied*. (See individual entries.)

ADP. Stands for Automatic Data Processing, referring to the manipulation of information by computer.

ALGOL. A programming language designed by an international committee. ALGOL was originally intended not as a programming language, but as a standard language for publishing *algorithms*. It has become very popular in Europe, and in the United States it has inspired a number of similar languages and influenced the development of others. ALGOL is best at mathematical and numerical problems.

Algorithm. An algorithm is a plan for solving a problem. It consists of a sequence of distinct, well-defined steps. Following the algorithm will always produce an answer in a finite number of steps. The procedure you use to multiply two numbers is an example. Devising algorithms and proving their correctness is an important part of programming.

Alphanumeric. A combination of alphabetic and numeric, meaning both letters and numbers.

American National Standards Institute. See *ANSI*.

American Standard Code for Information Interchange. See *ASCII*.

Analog. There are two main ways of doing things electronically. In the analog method, signals are continuously variable and the slightest change may be significant. Analog circuits are subject to *drift, distortion,* and *noise,* but they are capable of handling complex signals with relatively simple circuitry.

Analog computer. An analog computer handles numbers by representing them in the form of physical quantities such as light, pressure, heat, distance, angle, shaft speed, etc. (The word *analog* comes from *analogy.*) The most common sort of analog computer represents numbers as electrical voltages. It consists of a lot of special amplifiers with *patch* cords for connecting them together in various ways. Analog computers have been pretty much overshadowed by digital computers.

AND. This is one of the computer's logical operations. It causes the computer to compare two words *bit* by *bit.* The result is a "1" only if the first bit *and* the second bit are both "1." For example, 10110011 AND 11100101 give us 10100001.

AND gate. This is an electronic circuit whose output is a "1" only if all of the inputs are "1."

ANSI. Stands for the American National Standards Institute. They set up committees to study codes and computer languages and make recommendations that lead to greater uniformity in their use.

APL. A programming language designed to be used from interactive terminals. APL has a large number of very powerful mathematical operators, each represented by a special character. This, plus its very concise notation, makes an APL program look like a page from an alchemist's notebook. APL programs tend to be much shorter than programs written in other languages. APL is particularly good at handling *arrays.*

Application-oriented language. A programming language which is primarily useful in some specialized area.

Applications program. An applications program is one intended to solve a problem or do a job, as distinct from systems programs, which control the operations of the computer system.

Architecture. The organization of a computer's registers, memory elements, and other components is frequently referred to as its "architecture."

Argument. The number that a function works on to produce its results.

Arithmetic statement. An arithmetic statement includes an *expression* and a *variable* separated by an equals sign. The expression is evaluated and the resulting value is assigned to the variable.

Arithmetic unit. This is the part of the CPU that does the actual adding, subtracting, and shifting of numbers.

Array. The array is a very important type of *data structure*. We must often deal with a list of items that share some characteristic or are ordered in some way. We could give each a separate name, but it is more convenient to give each item a number corresponding to its place in the list and to give the list a name. Then we can refer to any item by its number or subscript. Such a list is a one-dimensional array, sometimes called a *vector*. Example: Array A has five members and it looks like this:

$$A_1, A_2, A_3, A_4, A_5$$

If each item in the group has two characteristics of interest, we can form a table of them. Each item now needs two identifying subscripts, one for its row and one for its column, so this is a two-dimensional array, often called a *matrix*. Example:

Array B $B_{11} \ B_{12} \ B_{13}$
2 rows, 3 columns $B_{21} \ B_{22} \ B_{23}$

We can have three-dimensional arrays, or even higher, depending on the computer language we are using. Many computer languages have special instructions for forming and manipulating arrays.

Artificial intelligence. This phrase is used to describe efforts to write programs that enable computers to play chess, prove theorems, recognize patterns, or do anything else which requires learning or reasoning.

ASCII. Stands for American Standard Code for Information Interchange (pronounced "ass-key") ASCII is a code for representing upper and lower case letters, numbers, symbols, and punctuation marks. Standardized by the industry, it is the code used by most computers and terminals (except in IBM equipment). (See Appendix, pp. 84–85.)

Assembler. An assembler is a program which translates instructions written in *assembly language* into *machine language*.

Assembly language. Assembly language is a great help to the programmer. It allows him to write his program using words like "LOAD," "JUMP," and "CLR" for instructions, instead of long strings of 1's and 0's. He can also refer to memory locations by symbolic names like "ALPHA" instead of *binary* numbers. The computer uses a program called an *assembler* to translate the commands into its own machine language. It also keeps track of the symbolic names and assigns appropriate memory locations to them. The assembler translates instructions on a one-for-one basis, so one instruction in assembly language becomes one instruction in machine language.

Assignment statement. The assignment statement is a basic part of all computer languages. It allows you to give a value to a variable. An example: X = 6.0. Keep in mind that the equals sign does not mean "equals" but "is replaced by." Otherwise you'll be startled by statements like "X = X + 1" which are perfectly legal.

Association for Computing Machinery (ACM). The major professional society for computer people.

Asynchronous. An asynchronous operation is one which does not proceed in step with some external timing.

Automatic Data Processing. See *ADP*.

Automatic programming. The idea that a computer could be used to simplify the job of writing programs was called "automatic programming" when it was first proposed. That work has resulted in the present *high-level languages*.

Background. Refers to a low-priority job that the computer works on when it isn't occupied by more pressing matters.

Backplane. This is the panel which all the circuit boards in a device plug into, and which contains all their interconnecting wiring.

Backus Normal Form. See *BNF*.

Base address. This *address* is the starting point for some manipulation which the computer must do in order to come up with the *effective address,* the address of the location it really wants.

BASIC. A programming language designed to be used from interactive terminals. BASIC is very easy to learn, having been originally designed as a beginner's language. In some respects it resembles a simplified FORTRAN. BASIC is the *high level language* most often supplied with small computers.

Batch processing. Letting a human being work directly with a computer results in a very inefficient use of the machine's time. While the human is typing or thinking what to do next, the computer is sitting expensively idle. Most early computer installations, therefore, allowed only batch processing. The programmer would submit his program and it would be run later as part of a batch of other programs. The next day the programmer would come in and get his results. If the program had fouled up, he would have another long wait before he could see the results of his corrected program. Batch processing makes good use of the computer's time, but it is a very inefficient way to develop programs. Today batch processing is used mostly for long programs that can be trusted to run properly.

Baud. A term used in describing data transmission rates: usually one *bit* per second.

BCD. Stands for Binary Coded Decimal, a common way of representing decimal numbers digitally. Here is a count to ten in BCD:

0		0000
1		0001
2		0010
3		0011
4		0100
5		0101
6		0110
7		0111
8		1000
9		1001
10	0001	0000

Each decimal digit is simply given its corresponding binary number. Notice that this code leaves six combinations unused (1010, 1011, 1100, 1101, 1110, 1111). In case any of them turn up by accident, we have to arrange the circuitry to ignore them.

Bidirectional bus. Refers to a *bus* that can carry signals in either direction. The bus also carries special signals that tell the devices connected to it which way data are passing.

Binary. The number system that computers use is called binary. It uses only two digits, 1 and 0. This is because the elec-

tronic circuits used in the computer have only two states: on
and off. Here are the numbers zero to sixteen in binary:

0	00000
1	00001
2	00010
3	00011
4	00100
5	00101
6	00110
7	00111
8	01000
9	01001
10	01010
11	01011
12	01100
13	01101
14	01110
15	01111
16	10000

Notice the pattern. Each place is twice the value of the place to
the right. At the very right is the 1's place; to the left of that is
the 2's place, then the 4's, the 8's, the 16's, the 32's, and so on.
Multiples of 2 end in zero. Notice that 1 is 1, 2 is 10, 4 is 100, 8
to 1000, 16 is 10000, and so forth.

Addition in binary is very simple:

$$0 + 0 = 0; 0 + 1 = 1; 1 + 0 = 1; \text{and } 1 + 1 = 10.$$

An example:

1001	9
+1100	+12
10101	21

Subtraction can be done in binary too, but that's another story.
(See *Two's complement.*)

Binary Coded Decimal. See *BCD.*

Binary search. The binary search is used when a computer must find the position of a symbol in an ordered list. The computer looks at the symbol halfway down the list and compares it with the symbol being searched for. It now knows which half of the list the symbol is in and can dismiss the other half. It repeats this process, eliminating half the possibilities each time until the desired symbol is found. This method is very efficient.

Binding time. The binding time is the stage at which a compiler replaces a symbolic name or address with its *machine language* form.

Bipolar. Refers to ordinary transistors and IC's, as distinct from MOS and CMOS components.

Bit. The smallest possible unit of information. One bit is enough to tell the difference between yes or no, up or down, on or off, one or zero; in short, any two opposites. Computers must represent information in the form of bits because the electronic circuits they are made of can have only two states: on or off.

Bit diddling. Sometimes storage efficiency can be greatly increased by packing extra information into unused parts of the computer word. Often the effort is more trouble than it's worth, and is scornfully referred to as "bit diddling."

Block. A section of information recorded on *magnetic tape* or *disk*. One block may consist of several records—collections of information consisting of one or more related items; or a record may extend over several blocks, depending on the characteristics of the device and the needs of the programmer.

Block diagram. A representation of a system, circuit, or program in which the individual functions are symbolized by labeled boxes and the relationships between them by connecting lines.

BNF. Stands for Backus Normal Form (or Backus-Naur

Form), a formal notation for defining the *syntax* of computer languages.

Bomb. A program "bombs" when it fails spectacularly. A programmer "bombs" a computer system when he deliberately writes a program that will disrupt the system.

Boolean algebra. A system of rules formulated by George Boole for expressing logical statements and manipulating them in an algebra-like way to establish them as true or false. Also known as "symbolic logic." It has direct application to the circuits used in computers.

Bootstrap loader. Since a computer must be programmed before it can accept information, and it can't be programmed until you can get information into it, how do you ever get the thing going? The answer is the bootstrap loader, a short program which is simple enough to be loaded manually by means of switches (or stored in read-only memory). It enables you to load a more complicated loader, which enables you to load your programs.

Branch. A branch instruction performs a test on a *register* or a *flag*. Depending on the results, the computer may continue with the next instruction or jump to a different part of the program. Branches are useful for performing decisions and constructing loops. See also *Conditional statement.*

Breakpoint. Some computers have a switch which will cause them to stop upon coming to a certain point in the program. The operator can then check the registers and memory to verify that the program is working properly. The same effect can also be achieved by putting "stop" instructions in the program. These are removed later when the program is correct.

Bubble sort. The bubble sort is a popular sorting *algorithm* for putting the elements of a file in order. As an example, assume we have a list of numbers that we want to place in descending order, largest first. Begin by comparing the first two numbers. If the first is larger than the second, leave them alone; otherwise exchange them. The first two numbers are now in correct order. Now compare the second and third numbers. Leave them alone if the second is larger than the third. If not, exchange them; then compare the second and first number once more, swapping them if necessary. The first three numbers are now in correct order. Compare the fourth number with the third. If the fourth number is smaller than the third, nothing happens. If the fourth number is larger, a series of comparisons and swaps moves it up into its proper place. This action resembles the behavior of a bubble in water—hence the name "bubble sort." The bubble sort is best used to sort small numbers of things. For large files, better sorting methods are available. See *Partition sort*.

Buffer. A buffer is a temporary storage area for data. It is often used when data transmission must take place at differing speeds. The buffer accumulates data from the slow device and then delivers the accumulated data in a spurt to the fast device.

Bug. A bug is an error in a program that keeps it from working properly.

Bus. In electronics, a bus is a power line that provides power to a large number of circuits. In computing, a bus is a group of wires that conveys information to a large number of devices. The information may be *data, commands,* or *addresses,* or all three in sequence. All the devices in the system are connected to the bus. Each device is continually listening for a command addressed to it. Only one device is allowed to transmit over the bus at once. Bus-oriented systems are becoming popular because they are flexible and easy to expand.

Byte. Originally defined as a subdivision of a long computer word, byte has come to mean a piece of information 8 *bits* long.

Cache memory. A high-speed memory capable of keeping up with the CPU. It acts as a buffer between the CPU and the slower main memory. Since the CPU is not slowed down by memory accesses, overall speed is increased.

CAI. Stands for Computer Aided Instruction. The computer leads the student through the subject step-by-step, asking questions as it goes. Depending on the pupil's response, the computer may go on to fresh material, go back over the lesson in more detail, or give the pupil a drill. CAI in its present form is likely to fade away when better computer systems become available, and the computer becomes a tool rather than a tutor. Students will then be able to explore the subject on their own, with the information handling abilities of the computer to assist them.

Calculator mode. Some *interactive systems* have a mode which allows the terminal to be used like a desk calculator. The user types an expression, and the computer evaluates it and returns the answer immediately. Also called fast answerback.

Card punch. The card punch is a piece of equipment that allows the computer to produce a deck of punched cards as output.

Card reader. A piece of equipment that takes a stack of punched cards and reads the information on them into the computer's memory, or onto magnetic tape or disk for future reference.

Card sorter. A piece of equipment that can take a stack of punched cards and sort them into alphabetic or numerical order.

Carry. When a computer adds two numbers and gets an answer too large to fit its registers, the leftmost "1" of the answer (the carry) is lost, but the computer recognizes this situation by setting its "carry" flag. What happens thereafter is up to the programmer.

Carry flag. See *Flag*.

Cathode Ray Tube. See *CRT.*

Central Processing Unit. See *CPU.*

Chaining. If a program is too big to fit into the memory, it is sometimes written in a series of segments. The computer works on one segment at a time. When it is done, it brings in the next segment, continuing in this way until the program is finished. This process is called chaining.

Character. A character is a small group of *bits* whose arrangement is given some definite meaning.

Character set. All the letters, numbers, and symbols used by a device or language.

Check sum. When a long block of data is transmitted to a computer, an extra word indicating the total number of bits is often attached. The computer keeps a running count and if the result does not agree with the check sum, it knows an error has been made.

Checkpoint. The status of a long-running program is often recorded at frequent intervals called checkpoints. If something goes wrong, the program can be restarted at its last checkpoint instead of from the beginning.

Chip. Refers to the tiny bit of silicon that forms the heart of an integrated circuit, or else to the entire integrated circuit.

Circularly-linked list. See *Ring.*

Clear. The process of setting the contents of a register, flag, or memory location to zero.

Clock. This is the master source of the computer's timing pulses. Everything proceeds in step with them.

Clustering. Refers to the process of grouping things with similar characteristics. A properly programmed computer can take a list of items and group them into clusters.

CMOS. Stands for Complementary *MOS*. An extension of MOS technology which produces integrated circuits with very low-power consumption.

COBOL. COBOL is a programming language designed specifically for business and data processing applications. It is widely used, despite suggestions that more modern languages could do the job more effeciently. COBOL strives for a natural, English-like appearance; and as a result, programs written in it tend to be very wordy. COBOL is very good at handling files.

Code. This can refer to a method of representing symbols in binary bits (as in ASCII or BCD) or to the lines of instructions making up a computer program. Programmers sometimes speak of "coding" or "writing code" when they are going through the final stage of writing down their programs.

Collating sequence. Every symbol and letter used by the computer can be considered to have a numerical value. It is this value that the computer uses when it sorts names. The collating sequence consists of all the letters, numbers, and symbols in order from lesser to greater.

COM. Short for Computer Output Microfilm. This device consists of a camera which takes pictures of a video screen. The result is a reel of microfilmed text.

Comments. Most high-level languages allow a programmer to put comments among his instructions. These comments are ignored by the computer. They make a program much easier to read and understand.

Compare. A computer instruction which effectively subtracts one word from another and indicates which of the two is larger.

Compiler. The compiler provides one of the ways of implementing a high-level language. The compiler is a program that translates each command into a series of instructions in machine language. This machine language program may be run at once, or saved for later. Once compiled, the program may be run as often as needed without further reference to the compiler.

Complement. A computer instruction that turns all the 1's in a word into 0's, and all the the 0's into 1's. For example, 10011011 complemented is 01100100.

Compute bound. A computer is said to be "compute bound" if the amount of work it can do is limited by the rate at which its CPU can perform calculations.

Computer. A computer is a device which manipulates data according to a series of instructions stored in its memory. By changing the instructions the computer can be made to do a completely different task. Thus the computer is probably the most general-purpose machine yet invented. It is important to note that both the instructions and the data are stored in the same memory and that both can be manipulated by the computer with equal ease. The individual operations performed by the modern electronic computer are very simple, but it does them at the rate of thousands per second, enabling complex tasks to be finished in a remarkably short time.

Computer Aided Instruction. See *CAI*.

Computer languages. The only instructions that computers understand are strings of 1's and 0's. This is known as *machine language*. Programming in machine language is very tedious, so various computer languages have been devised to make programming computers easier. The first of these is *assembly language,* which frees the programmer from the need to think in 1's and 0's. Then there are *high- level languages,* which give the programmer the ability to write programs almost as easily as normal English.

Computer operator. The computer operator sits at a console in the midst of the cabinets that make up the computer. He changes disks and tapes, keeps an eye on the screens and lights that show what the computer is doing, aborts programs that go wrong, and restarts the computer when some foul-up causes it to stop working.

Computer Output Microfilm. See *COM*.

Computer science. The art of solving problems with computers. Notice that it concerns itself as much with finding ways to solve problems as it does with computers.

Concatenation. This is the name of an operation in which the computer takes two *strings* and links them together, making one long string out of them.

Concentrator. Using the phone lines to communicate with a distant computer can become expensive if there is a lot of computer use. A concentrator saves money by combining the data from several local lines and sending it out over a single high-speed data line.

Conditional statement. This statement causes the computer to check something and use that as a basis for choosing among alternative courses of action. Same as a *branch*. Also called an IF statement.

Console. A panel containing the indicator lights, switches, and video screens needed by the operator to control the computer and keep an eye on its operation.

Constant. Any number you don't expect to change. Instead of giving it a variable name, it can be written into the program explicitly. It's wise to make sure that you won't ever want to change it before you do this.

Contention. Occurs when two CPU's attempt to control the same device at once.

Context switching. If a computer must alter its behavior suddenly, in response to an *interrupt,* for example, it has to "save" its registers by storing their old contents in a safe place before going to the new routine. This takes time. But if the computer is built so that it can use a section of memory as its registers, or if it has an extra set of registers, it can have two different programs stored away and go from one to another just by jumping to a different part of memory. This is called context switching.

Control unit. The part of the CPU that interprets instructions and generates appropriate signals to the other parts of the computer.

Conversational. Synonymous with *interactive.*

Conversational compiler. See *Incremental compiler.*

Conversion error. If you tell a computer to multiply 0.0001 ten thousand times, you are likely to get not 1.0, but something like .999998. This is because the computer cannot represent all fractions exactly in binary. Some fractions continue indefinitely when translated into binary and get cut off short by the computer's limited word length. Smart programmers try to use fractions like 1/2, 1/4, 1/8, 1/16, etc. because these can be represented exactly in binary, thus avoiding conversion error.

Core memory. A core is a tiny doughnut of magnetic material. It can be magnetized in either of two directions, so a single core is capable of storing one bit. Woven into webs of wires, cores made up the main memory of most computers until recently. Even though cores have been largely replaced by semiconductor memories, many people still say "core memory" when talking about the main memory of the computer.

Cps. Stands for "characters per second" when speaking of data transmission. Not to be confused with "cycles per second."

CPU. Short for Central Processing Unit. This contains all the registers, arithmetic circuitry, comparators, and so forth that do the actual work of computing.

Crash. A computer system is said to crash when it stops working for some reason and must be restarted by the operator.

CRT. Stands for Cathode Ray Tube. This is the technical name of the picture tube in your TV set or the video terminal.

Cursor. A cursor is a mark that a video terminal makes on its screen, showing where the next character will go (so you won't lose your place).

Cybercrud. A word coined by Theodore Nelson to describe the use of computers to "put things over on people." It includes such things as attaching the word "computer" or "computerized" to something to impress people; blaming "the computer" for your mistakes; forcing people to put up with badly thought out systems because "the computer has to have it this way." Cybercrud will last only as long as the general public knows little about computers.

Cybernetics. The study of communication and control in information handling systems, both natural and artificial.

Cycle. See *Ring*.

Cycle stealing. Suspending the operation of a CPU for one operation cycle in order to allow time for some slow process to finish.

Cycle time. The time needed for a CPU to go through a complete operation cycle.

Cylinder. A cylinder is composed of all the corresponding *tracks* on a set of disks. There are as many concentric cylinders as there are tracks on one disk. Since the read/write *heads* for the disks move in unison, they look at all the tracks of a particular cylinder at once. By organizing information in terms of cylinders, the need to move the heads is reduced.

D/A converter. This device converts digital information to analog form.

Data. The information that the computer manipulates is called data. Data can be just about anything that can be expressed as patterns or numbers.

Data base. If you are going to manipulate data, you need data to work with. The data that the computer must have for some particular manipulation is called the data base. For a payroll accounting program, the data base consists of the employees' names, pay rate, etc.

Data channel. A data channel is a small computer buried inside a large computer. It handles data communications for the big computer, freeing its time for more worthwhile things.

Data link. A data link is some way of rapidly transferring data from one place to another. It can be a telephone line, a coaxial cable, a radio or microwave link, or even a laser beam.

Data processing. Most of the applications encountered in business involve many input and output operations, with the computer spending comparatively little of its time doing calculations. A term often applied to this situation is data processing.

Data structure. The decision on how data are to be organized in memory and referred to by the computer is an important one. Picking the proper data structure can simplify the computer's job greatly. Some data structures often encountered are *files, lists, arrays, stacks,* and *queues.*

Deadlock. A deadlock occurs in a computer system when two devices each want to use something that the other device has reserved. This brings everything to a screeching halt. The solution is to allocate resources on a priority basis or to have some kind of tie-breaking circuitry.

Debugging. The process of finding and correcting errors—*bugs*—in a program so it will work as intended.

Decimal. The ordinary 10-based number system we are used to using every day. In the early days of computing, a few computers were made that used decimal arithmetic internally, and these were called decimal machines.

Decrement. To decrease (usually by one).

Dedicated. A piece of equipment is said to be dedicated if it is assigned to one particular use only. Minicomputers are often dedicated. Microprocessors are intended to be dedicated.

Default. Some programs or systems allow you a choice of several options. If you do not pick one, one is automatically assigned, by default.

Delimiter. A special character or word used in program statements to indicate to the computer that a particular section has begun or ended. Instead of analyzing the whole statement to pick out its parts, the computer just looks for the delimiters.

Destructive read. Describes a memory element in which the act of reading data from a memory location erases it. To keep the information in that memory location, it must be rewritten after it has been read. Magnetic core memory is the chief example of this.

Diagnostic check. A program that puts the computer through its paces in an attempt to detect a malfunction.

Diagnostic message. If you misplace or leave out a punctuation mark when writing your program, or make some other error in the form of the language, the computer will not be able to run your program. It won't even try. Instead it will return your program with diagnostic messages indicating what is wrong so that you will be able to fix up your program and try again.

Digital. There are two main ways of doing things electronically. The digital method is to consider a circuit either on or off, a signal as either present or absent, with no levels in between. Electronic circuits using the digital mode are simple to design and non-critical in operation. The all-or-nothing nature of digital circuits makes them immune to drift and distortion, and their simplicity makes them easy to make in large numbers.

Digital computer. A device for doing calculations or manipulating data that works by counting instead of making measurements, as an *analog computer* does.

Digitize. To transform a signal or piece of information into digital form.

DIP. Stands for Dual Inline Package, the form in which most integrated circuits are made. Its two parallel rows of pins make it look not unlike a caterpillar.

Direct access. See *Random access.*

Direct address. An *address* which does not require any manipulation by the computer.

Direct lookup. In order to use this search technique, each item in the file must have an identifying key. There is a direct relation between the value of a key and the position of an item in the file. To find a given item, all the search program needs to do is to calculate the value of its key. This is a very fast process. Its drawback is that it wastes memory space if there are a large number of empty positions in the file. To overcome this, methods of *key transformation* (or *hashing*) are used.

Direct Memory Access. See *DMA*.

Disabled. A device which has been given a signal that prevents it from functioning is said to be disabled.

Discrete circuitry. Building electronic circuits by soldering together individual parts produces what has come to be known as discrete circuitry (as opposed to the use of *integrated circuits*). Discrete components have been largely replaced by integrated circuits because discrete circuitry is bulkier, more expensive to assemble, and less reliable.

Disk. A magnetic disk is a thin disk of magnetic material capable of storing a large amount of information. It spins rapidly, and *heads* similar to heads in tape recorders read and write information onto concentric tracks.

Disk drive. A disk drive houses several magnetic disks, keeps them spinning, and moves the read/write heads into proper position when information must be read from or stored on the disk.

Disk pack. A stack of disks joined together, so that they can be replaced or removed from a disk drive as a single unit.

Diskette. See *Floppy Disk*.

Displacement. The displacement is a number which a computer must add to a *base address* to form an *effective address*.

Distributive sort. A sorting procedure that divides the data elements into two or more distinct groups or subsets. The *partition sort* is an example.

Documentation. When a programmer has a working program, his last job is to document it. Documentation includes the program's name, its purpose, its input and output requirements, possibly notes on the algorithm or data structure used, and so on. Good documentation is essential if anyone else is ever going to try to understand or change the program. Even the original programmer will be sorry if he has to work on a program he failed to document six months earlier.

Down. Said of a computer that is not running. It may be shut down for maintenance; there may be a hardware failure; or the operating system may have been deranged by a runaway program.

DMA. Stands for Direct Memory Access. When large amounts of data must be transferred to or from a peripheral device, it speeds things up if the CPU temporarily surrenders control of memory to the *peripheral*. This is faster than funneling all the data through the CPU.

Drift. A change in the properties of an electrical circuit, as a result of aging or temperature changes.

Dual Inline Package. See *DIP*.

Dummy. A dummy statement is one that does not cause the computer to do anything. It merely serves as a place to attach a label which is needed as a reference point.

Duplex. A communications line that can send data in both directions at once is said to be a full-duplex line. A line that can send in either direction but not both at once is a half-duplex line. Duplex can also refer to a computer system that contains two interconnected CPU's.

Dynamic. Refers to a process occuring during program execution.

EBCDIC. Stands for Extended Binary Coded Decimal Interchange Code (pronounced "eb-see-dick"). EBCDIC is the code used to represent information in most IBM equipment. It is closely related to the code used on punched cards, which may explain IBM's reluctance to shift to ASCII.

Echo. When data are being transmitted, the receiving device often re-transmits or "echoes back" the information so that the originating device can be sure it was received correctly.

EDP. Stands for Electronic Data Processing, referring to the manipulation of information by computer.

Effective address. With some addressing modes, the computer must perform some calculations to come up with the address of the memory location it is really interested in. This is known as the effective address. See also *Base address*.

Electronic Data Processing. See *EDP*.

Emulation. The general-purpose nature of computers is illustrated by the fact that a computer can be programmed to imitate another computer. A small computer can emulate a larger, more powerful computer. Programs written for one machine can be run on another. Designs can be tested for computers that haven't even been built yet. The biggest drawback is that the computer performing the emulation is slowed down drastically.

Enabled. A device which has been given a signal that permits it to function is said to be enabled.

Error correcting codes. There are codes for information transmission that make it possible not only to detect errors, but to fix them as well. This involves sending extra information along with each word, with a corresponding reduction in the transmission rate.

Error detecting codes. If a single *bit* is wrong, the computer can make a hash of things. For this reason, codes for transmitting information often include some means of detecting errors. The most common is the inclusion of a *parity* bit in each word.

Error message. When writing a program it is a good idea to assume that the user will make mistakes. The program should check for these mistakes and print error messages when they appear so that the user will know what he is doing wrong.

Escape key. This is a key found on some keyboards. When pressed, it redefines all the other keys, giving them new meanings. This allows the use of special characters or codes not normally found on the keyboard. May also be called "alternate."

Etched circuit. See *Printed circuit.*

Even parity. See under *Parity.*

Exception report. Instead of filling reams of paper with routine items, a computer can be asked to produce an exception report, which shows only the items falling outside normal bounds. Much easier to read.

Exclusive OR. This is one of the computer's logical operations. It compares two words bit by bit. If both bits are the same, the result is a "0." If both bits are different, the result is a "1." It follows the rule "either, but not both." For instance, 10101100 exclusively OR'ed with 00111010 gives us 10010110.

Exclusive OR gate. This is an electronic circuit whose output is a "1" if its two inputs are different, and a "0" if they are the same. Notice that this follows the rules for binary addition if carries are disregarded. For this reason, the exclusive OR gate is sometimes known as a "half adder."

Executive. A program that helps to manage the operation of a computer system. (See *Operating system.*)

Expression. An expression consists of anything from a single constant or variable to the most complicated arrangement of operators and functions that can be fitted into a single program statement. It does not, however, contain an equals sign.

Extended Binary Coded Decimal Interchange Code. See *EBCDIC.*

Fast answerback. See *Calculator mode.*

Field. A field is a subdivision of a *record,* usually consisting of a single item of information related to the rest of the record. A punched card is often divided into several fields.

Field engineer. Fancy title for the repairman whom the manufacturer sends to fix your computer when it stops working.

FIFO. Stands for "first in, first out." This is how things are managed in a *queue.*

File. A file consists of a collection of *records.* Each record has a number corresponding to its position in the file.

First generation. Refers to the computers of the early 1950's that used vacuum tubes.

Fixed point arithmetic. In fixed point arithmetic, the computer considers the decimal point to be fixed at a certain point in the computer word. (The point is often fixed at the far left hand of the word, so that the computer treats all numbers as fractions.) This is done to simplify the arithmetic routines. If the programmer wants the decimal point some place else, he must apply a correction factor to both the input and output.

Flag. A flag is a single bit of memory that the CPU uses to keep track of certain conditions. A typical example is the carry flag, which is set to 1 whenever a carry occurs during an addition. By testing the carry flag, the arithmetic routines know when a carry has occurred and can take appropriate action. Most computers have several flags.

Flip-flop. An electronic circuit which has only two stable states. It can be made to switch states by a pulse on its input. One flip-flop can store one bit of information.

Floating point arithmetic. The size of the numbers that a computer can handle is limited by its word length. An 8 bit word, for instance, cannot handle numbers larger than 255. To get around this, numbers are represented as a fraction multiplied by a power of ten. (This system is often used by scientists and engineers and is called *scientific notation*.) For example, 9265 would be .9265 × 10^4. (Or, since computer printers can't deal with superscripts, it would probably look more like .9265 E4.)

The computer word is broken into two parts. One part contains the fractional part of the number, the other the exponent of the power of ten. Precision is sacrificed, since the fractional part can take up only part of the word. However, very large and very small numbers can be expressed this way. Because the effective position of the decimal point changes when the exponent is changed, this system is called floating point.

Floppy disk. The floppy disk (or more properly, diskette) was developed to give small computer systems an inexpensive and convenient means of storing information. It is the general shape and size of a 45 rpm phonograph record. Despite its name, it isn't really floppy, although it is flexible when compared to the disks used on large computers.

Flow chart. This is the traditional way of diagramming programs. Instructions are written into little rectangles, and choice points or branches are diamonds. Lines connect them together, showing the flow of control from one part of the program to another. Flow charts are not strictly necessary, but they can be helpful in visualizing how a program works.

Foreground. A program which has priority over other programs is said to be "in the foreground."

Format. Usually refers to the arrangement of the computer's output. Most programming languages give the programmer some control over the way the output will appear on the printed page.

FORTRAN. FORTRAN is probably the most widely known computer language. It was developed primarily for the sort of calculation found in scientific and technical applications. FORTRAN was the first language easy enough to learn such that users could write their own programs instead of depending on professional programmers. Expressions in FORTRAN have a strong resemblance to ordinary algebra. FORTRAN's chief defect is its lack of character-handling facilities.

Free format. Many languages allow the programmer considerable freedom in the way he arranges his instructions on a page, the computer being programmed to ignore superfluous blanks. This can be used to great advantage to indent related statements, making the program easier to read and understand.

Front end. This is a small computer that stands between a group of terminals and the main computer. It handles communications, error checking, and other minor jobs that are not worth the time of the big computer.

Full-duplex line. See *Duplex*.

Function. A function is a special subroutine kept in the computer's memory. You can call it by writing its name in a program statement, just as though it were another operator. Functions typically available include square root, log, absolute value, and trig functions. Some computer languages allow users to define their own functions.

Garbage collection. Some programs have the computer filling up its memory space with things that are referred to once and then not needed again. To conserve valuable memory space, routines are written to clear out obsolete information. This is called garbage collection.

Gate. A gate is a digital circuit which produces an output only for certain conditions of input. Each of the simple logic functions, such as AND, OR, NAND, NOT, can be performed by the corresponding gate. More complex functions can be made by wiring gates together. (See Appendix, p. 86.)

GIGO. Stands for "garbage in, garbage out." A reminder that no program can produce good results with faulty data.

Glitch. A glitch is a bit of electrical noise that causes circuits to misbehave. By extension, the term refers to any minor but irritating foul-up.

Global variable. A global variable is one that is available to all the sections of a multi-part program.

Go to. See *Jump.*

Graph. A graph structure is the most general type of linked list. Its structure can include closed loops, or *rings,* and multiple branches, or *trees,* as well as ordinary sequential lists.

Half adder. See *Exclusive OR gate.*

Half-duplex line. See *Duplex.*

Hand calculation. This is a method for checking the correctness of programs. The programmer goes through the program, performing each instruction as if he were the computer. Hand calculation is very tedious, so it is usually used only on very simple routines, or to check just the general structure of large programs.

Handshaking. When a machine transmits data to another machine, it usually ends each transmission with a signal that means "Did you get that O.K.?" And the other machine answers with a signal that means "Yes I did, what's next?" or "Please repeat that" This continual exchange is called "handshaking."

Hard copy. Information in a form that you can carry away with you.

Hardware. Refers to the physical equipment, the actual nuts and bolts and wiring, that makes up a computer. If a particular bit of data manipulation is handled by circuitry rather than by a program, it is said to be "in hardware." Doing things in hardware is fast but usually expensive, so it is reserved for things that are done very frequently and would take up a lot of time if handled by a program.

Hardware language. The limitations of terminals, printers, and other hardware can impose restrictions on the implementation of a programming language. The hardware language is a form of the language which is suitable for direct input to a computer.

Hash clash. A "hash clash" occurs when a *key transformation* or hashing operation results in two different items being given the same key. One way around this is to re-hash the second item until it finally gets a unique key.

Hashing. See *Key transformation*.

Head. A small electromagnet (similar to the heads in home tape recorders) used to read or write information onto the magnetic surface of a tape, disk, or drum.

Head crash. This is a serious failure in a disk or drum unit. The read/write heads drop onto the surface of the spinning disk or drum, scratching and gouging it beyond repair.

Heuristic. This refers to a problem-solving technique in which general principles and rules of thumb are used to approach a solution. Unlike an algorithm, the heuristic approach does not guarantee a solution. However, heuristic methods can result in a faster and simpler solution, and where algorithms are not available, they are often the only resource.

Hexadecimal. A number system which uses 16 digits. Since we don't have that many normal digits available, we have to fill out with letters. Here we count to 16 in decimal, hexadecimal, and binary:

Decimal	Hexadecimal	Binary
0	0	0000
1	1	0001
2	2	0010
3	3	0011
4	4	0100
5	5	0101
6	6	0110
7	7	0111
8	8	1000
9	9	1001
10	A	1010
11	B	1011
12	C	1100
13	D	1101
14	E	1110
15	F	1111
16	10	10000

If we take a long binary number and separate it into groups of four bits, we can substitute a hexadecimal digit for each group and get an instant translation of binary into hex. For example, 1011001010000111 binary is B287 in hexadecimal. Hex is a very compact way of representing binary numbers and especially convenient when the word length is a multiple of four.

High-level language. High-level languages, or programming languages, were developed to make the task of programming easier. Some widely used high-level languages are BASIC, FORTRAN, ALGOL, COBOL, and PL/I. Instead of writing his program in the tedious detail required by machine or assembly language, the programmer can write English-like instructions which the computer then translates into machine language. There are many advantages. The programmer is relieved of the need to know the intimate details of the computer.

High-level languages are easy to learn. Programs become easier to read and understand. Because one statement in a higher-level language takes the place of many machine language instructions, programs become more concise. Overall programming time is shortened. The user gets a notation that is related to his problem, rather than the structure of the computer. Completed programs can be run with only minor changes on other computers.

There are some disadvantages, too. Because the computer must translate the program before it can be run, there is a penalty in computer time. The programs produced are seldom as efficient as those written in machine language. Because programming languages have their strong and weak points, they are not as universal as machine language.

Hollerith. This can refer to the information on punched cards (Hollerith fields), to the code they are punched in (Hollerith code), or to the cards themselves (Hollerith cards). As you might guess, Hollerith did much work on early punched card tabulating equipment.

Housekeeping. The time that the computer spends clearing flags and registers, rewinding tapes, and doing other neatening and tidying is called housekeeping.

IC. Short for *integrated circuit.*

Identifier. An identifier is a combination of letters and/or numbers used as a name for a variable, a function, a procedure, or as a statement label. Different languages have different rules about what combinations of symbols can serve as identifiers. You can name a variable after almost anything, but it is better practice to choose a name that relates to the job at hand.

IF statement. See *Conditional statement.*

Image. When information is transferred directly from one medium to another without transformation or manipulation, the result is an image.

Implementation dependent. Refers to extended or non-standard features of a programming language that are available only on a particular computer system. The use of implementation-dependent features can cause problems if the program must be run on a different computer.

Implied addressing. An addressing mode in which no actual *address* is involved. For instance, if a computer has only a single accumulator, all instructions which refer to the accumulator need not have any address at all, because there is no possibility of confusion. Such instructions are said to have implied addressing.

Increment. To increase (usually by one).

Incremental compiler. The incremental compiler stands halfway between the *compiler* and the *interpreter*. It compiles instructions one at a time, making it possible to modify, insert, or delete an instruction without the need to recompile the entire program. Also called an on-line, interactive, or conversational compiler.

Index. See under *Loop.*

Indexed addressing. An addressing mode in which the computer finds the address of the desired memory location by referring to an index register. By successively adding or subtracting one to this index register, the computer can be made to step through a list or table.

Indirect addressing. An addressing mode in which the instruction refers to a memory location which contains the address of the memory location that has the desired data.

Information retrieval. The art of storing information so that it may be recovered easily. Branches include abstracting, locating facts of interest, and language translation.

Initialize. To set program variables to their starting values at the beginning of a program or subroutine.

Input. This is information from the outside world which must be put into the computer to accomplish some task. Common input devices include video terminals, teletypewriters, card readers, paper tape readers, and magnetic tape drives.

Instruction register. A register in the CPU that contains the instruction currently being executed.

Instruction set. The group of simple commands that a computer is capable of performing.

Integer arithmetic. An integer is an ordinary number with no fractional part. In integer arithmetic, the computer ignores any fractions that turn up. For instance, eight divided by three would be two.

Integrated circuit (IC). An integrated circuit is a tiny chip of silicon several millimeters square that has been subjected to a series of diffusions and etchings resulting in the equivalent of several thousand interconnected transistors. IC's can be made that perform very complex functions. Their small size and low cost have made possible a dramatic jump in computer performance.

Intelligent terminal. This is a rather vague term for a terminal that does anything but just send and receive data from a computer. Some terminals have *microprocessors* built into them so they can do some data manipulations on their own, thereby saving the time of the big computer. We can expect to hear about intelligent this and intelligent that as microprocessors show up in more different pieces of equipment.

Interactive. Refers to a program or system that can ask questions of the user and then take action based on his response. "Conversational" is often used to mean the same thing.

Interactive compiler. See *Incremental compiler.*

Interface. It often happens that it is necessary to connect two devices that do not "speak each other's language." The solution is to provide an interface, which transforms the signals passing between them so that each device hears what it is used to.

Interpreted card. When the information contained on a punched card is printed across the top so you can read it, the card is said to be "interpreted."

Interpreter. The interpreter is one of the ways of implementing a high-level computer language. The interpreter is a program that causes the computer to scan each instruction, decide what it is being told to do, and then do it. Each time the program is run, it must be interpreted all over again. Interpreters are best for programs that will only be run once or twice, or that get changed a lot. Most of the languages designed to be used from terminals are interpretive.

Interrupt. It often happens that while a computer is working on a problem it is desirable to have it stop and do something else for a while. This is called an interrupt. When a computer is interrupted, it stops, stores the address of its current instruction and the contents of its flags and registers, identifies the nature of the interrupt, then goes to an appropriate interrupt routine. When it has finished handling the interrupt, the computer restores the information it had saved earlier and takes up where it left off.

Interrupt priority. Some computers have several interrupt lines, each with a different priority. The devices whose needs are most important are connected to the higher priority lines. A high-priority device can interrupt an interrupt from a low-priority device, but if a high-priority interrupt is being processed, lower priority devices must wait.

Inverter. In logic circuits, an inverter is a circuit whose output is the inverse of its input. A "1" gives a "0" and vice versa. In talking of power supplies, an inverter is a circuit that changes DC into AC.

I/O. Short for input/output.

I/O bound. A computer is said to be I/O bound if its CPU spends most of its time waiting for *input* or *output* devices to finish instead of doing calculations. This happens because the CPU is so much faster than I/O devices.

I/O volume. The physical component of an I/O device on which data are recorded (such as a reel of tape, disk pack, etc.).

IOCS. Stands for Input/Output Control System. It's part of the *operating system*.

Iteration. Repetition.

Job. A program as submitted to the computer. A job consists of a program plus extra information that tells the computer which is program and which is data, who to bill, what language is being used, and so on.

Job stream. A succession of programs set up so that the computer can proceed from one to the next without the need for operator intervention.

Jump. A computer instruction that tells the computer *not* to look for its next instruction in the next memory location, but to go somewhere else instead. An example: if the computer has just finished an instruction at location 1000 and it finds a "jump to 1050" instruction in location 1001, it puts 1050 in its program counter. This causes it to go to location 1050 for its next instruction, ignoring everything in between. Another name for the jump instruction is "go to."

K. In electronics, "K" is short for "kilo," a prefix meaning one thousand. In the computer world, K means 1024. This number is a convenient point of reference because it is a power of two and very close to one thousand. If you hear someone talking about "8K of memory," what he means is 8 × 1024, or 8192.

Key to disk. Used to describe a system that lets you type information on a keyboard and store it directly on a magnetic disk, bypassing the medium of punched cards.

Key to tape. Used to describe a system in which information typed on a keyboard goes directly onto a magnetic tape, bypassing the medium of punched cards.

Key transformation. When a file has a large number of empty positions, there is a waste of memory space. The solution is to use a smaller file; but now the keys or names used to identify the individual items in the file will no longer relate to their position in the file. To get around this, the original keys are transformed or "hashed" by a simple operation that will result in a new set of keys that will fit into the smaller file. To find an item, the search program calculates the key as before, then performs the transformation on it to get the new key, which gives the position of the item in the file.

Keyboard. Most input devices have a keyboard. It is usually patterned after a typewriter keyboard, though some of the keys may have special characters or commands or unusual symbol pairings.

Keypunch. The keypunch is a piece of equipment for punching information onto computer cards from a keyboard.

Kilo. A prefix meaning one thousand. One kilobaud equals one thousand baud.

Kludge. A kludge (rhymes with "sludge") is an improvised lashup often involving adhesive tape and string. It works fine, but only as long as it's pampered, and no one trips over a wire.

Label. This is a number or letter or a name you give to a program statement so that the computer can find it later.

Large Scale Integration. See *LSI*.

Latch. Many signals inside a computer are transitory. A latch is a circuit which, when triggered, stores whatever appears on its inputs and holds it for later use.

Latency time. This is the time it takes a disk unit to find a specific piece of information on a given track.

Library. Every computer has a collection of programs for doing routine tasks. Familiarity with the program library can save a lot of work.

LIFO. Stands for "last in, first out." This is how things are managed in a *stack*.

Light pen. This looks like a bulky pen with a cable attached; it can detect the presence of light when held to a video screen. Depending on the program, a light pen can be used to draw things, point to things, or move things around on the screen.

Line printer. A piece of equipment that prints out information on wide sheets of paper, a full line at a time. The line printer is very fast and very noisy and eats a box of paper in next to no time. Even so, it's not fast enough to keep up with the computer.

Linear. Resembling a straight line, without bends or kinks. A linear function can be graphed as a straight line. Linear amplifiers produce no distortion. Integrated circuits are divided into two broad groups, digital and linear (meaning analog.)

Linear search. See *Sequential search*.

Link bit. Some computers have a link bit (or *flag*) which allows two registers to be combined and used as one double-length register.

Linkage editor. This program binds portions of programs

and subroutines together into complete, executable programs by knitting together the cross references between them.

Linking loader. A linking loader takes several routines and loads them into memory as a single program, taking care of the cross references between them and relocating as necessary.

LISP. A programming language which grew out of the artificial intelligence field, where it finds most of its adherents. It uses an unusual notation peppered with parentheses. Some insist that "LISP" stands for "Lots of Irritating Single Parentheses." LISP is best at general symbol manipulation and list processing.

List. A list (or, more properly, a linked list) is a data structure in which each item of information has attached to it one or more *links* or *pointers* which refer to other items. (Also called a "chained" or "threaded" list.) Note that the relationships between the items can be much more complicated that the simple sequence that we usually have in mind when we speak of a list (which is known as a "linear linked list"). We can have *rings* or *trees* or some combination of all of these (a *graph*).

List language. A language that is designed to be good at manipulating data in the form of lists. Examples include SNOBOL and LISP. List languages often look strange.

Literal. This is the name or symbol that stands for nothing more than itself.

Load and go. A mode of operation in which programs are loaded and immediately executed.

Load module. This is a section of program that can be loaded into main memory and executed.

Loader. A loader is a program which accepts input from an external device and places it in memory. The simplest loaders do no more than this. Other loaders include *relocating loaders, linking loaders,* and *bootstrap loaders.*

Local. Refers to equipment at your own location. As minicomputers and microprocessors become cheaper and more numerous, more people will be able to do their computing locally.

Local variable. A local variable is one that is used by only one part of a multi-part program, and not by any of the others.

Logic. A logical variable represents something that is either true or false. If true it is given the value 1; if false, the value 0. Logical operators include AND, OR, and NOT. A AND B has a value of 1 (true) if both A *and* B are 1; otherwise A AND B = 0. A OR B has a value of 1 if either A *or* B is 1. The NOT operator gives you the reverse of a logical variable. If A = 1, then NOT A = 0. Logical expressions can be built up from variables, relational operators, and logical operators. A ≠ B, L AND (M OR N), are expressions whose truth or falsity can be established. Logical expressions are often used in conditional *branch* statements such as: IF D ≥ L OR C = 0, GO TO 17.

There are also machine language instructions which cause the computer to perform AND or OR operations on strings of bits.

In the hardware domain, there are circuits called *gates* which perform logic functions and which can be hooked together to produce complex logic functions.

Log-in. The process of getting the computer to recognize you, so you can use the system from your terminal.

Loop. A loop is a series of instructions that the computer performs over and over. When it gets to the end, it finds a *jump* instruction telling it to go to the beginning. The computer can be made to go through the loop any number of times. Here is a sample "program" that will do something six times and stop:

    1   Load 6 into "Index"
    2   Body of loop:
    .   Something we want
    .   done six times

    7 Subtract 1 from "Index"
    8 Skip if "Index" is zero
    9 Go to 2
   10 Stop

"Index" is a memory location we use to keep track of how many times we have been through the loop. Each time the computer completes the loop, it subtracts one from "Index." Then it tests the value of "Index" with a *branch* instruction. If the job is not finished, the computer goes on to instruction 9, which tells it to go back to the beginning. But if the loop has been done six times, "Index" will be zero and the computer will skip over instruction 9 and find instruction 10, which tells it to stop. (Another section of the program might have followed at this point, rather than a "stop" instruction.) Some means must always be provided to get out of the loop, or else the computer will go round and round forever (or until someone gets impatient and kills your program).

LSI. Stands for Large Scale Integration, the technology which makes it possible to produce CPU's and other such complex circuits in a single integrated circuit.

Machine dependent. Anything which makes use of features unique to a certain computer is said to be machine dependent.

Machine independent. Does not rely on the features of a particular computer; can be generalized to all computers.

Machine language. A program written in the basic, simple instructions that the computer understands directly is said to be in machine language. Such programs take up little space in memory and run in a minimum of time, but they are extremely tedious to write and debug. One reason is that each instruction is a string of 1's and 0's that is very difficult to remember. Another is that it takes a large number of these instructions to accomplish most tasks, since the computer has to be told what to do on a word-by-word basis.

Machine readable. Capable of being translated into the electronic signals that the computer understands.

Macro. When writing programs in *assembly language,* certain sequences of instructions tend to occur frequently. It is very convenient to be able to give such a sequence a symbolic name and arrange for the assembler to insert those instructions whenever it finds the name in a program. The name that calls up this sequence is called a macro instruction, and assemblers with this capability are macro assemblers.

Magnetic disk. See *disk*.

Magnetic tape. A popular medium for storing large amounts of information that doesn't have to be referred to frequently. Magnetic tape is wider and made to tighter specifications than the tape in your home tape recorder, but otherwise it's very similar.

Main frame. The cabinet or piece of equipment in a computer system that contains the CPU.

Mask. It sometimes happens that we are interested in only part of a computer word. We can get rid of the rest by masking it out with an AND operation. For instance, if we want to look at only the last two bits of an eight-bit word, we AND it with 00000011. This makes the first six bits of the word zeroes and leaves the rest unchanged.

Mass memory. A computer often has to handle large amounts of data, much more than it has room for in its main memory. This is stored in mass memory, usually on magnetic tape or disk. Getting data from mass memory is a lot slower than from main memory; but hopefully the computer does not need to look at this information very often.

Mathematical model. An idealized conception of some process, capable of being expressed in mathematical terms.

Matrix. A matrix is a two dimensional *array,* or table of numbers. In the hardware domain, a matrix can be anything arranged in a grid-like pattern.

Mean Time Between Failures. See *MTBF.*

Mega. A prefix meaning one million. One megabyte equals one million *bytes.*

Memory. The memory of a computer is where it finds its instructions and the data it is to work with; also where it stores its results. Memory is organized as a series of locations or cells, each of which can hold one word. The computer can read a word from a memory location, or it can store a new word there (in which case the old contents are lost). The locations are numbered in sequence. These numbers or *addresses* enable the computer to refer to the memory.

Memory dump. A print-out of the contents of the computer's memory. Unless you know exactly what to look for, a dump is very difficult to interpret. Usually used only in desperation.

Memory mapped I/0. Computers made in this way do not have separate instructions for input and output. Instead, external devices look like locations in the computer's memory, and the computer uses its memory reference instructions to communicate with them.

Memory protection. Sometimes valuable information is lost when it is overwritten by a runaway program that has jumped out of its allotted bounds through some error. To keep this from happening, memory can be put into a "protect" mode, so that it may be read from but not written into.

Merge. To combine two files into one while keeping the original order.

Metalanguage. A language that is used to talk about other languages (programming languages in this case) is a metalanguage.

Metaprogram. A program that is designed to process other programs as input is called a metaprogram. Examples include *assemblers, compilers,* and *operating systems.*

Microcomputer. This rather useless term is sometimes used to describe any computer built around a *microprocessor.* As microprocessors become more powerful and more widely used, it will probably go out of use.

Microprocessor. Recent advances in integrated circuit-making have made it possible to put highly complex functions in a package the size of a domino. The microprocessor was born when semiconductor manufacturers decided to make what amounted to a CPU on a single chip. The idea was that such a chip could be used as a universal process controller, replacing large amounts of complex circuitry in all sorts of equipment. Interesting things began happening when people started building little computers around microprocessors. Now microprocessors are designed with computing in mind, and some are directly modeled after existing minicomputers.

Micro-programming. A micro-programmed CPU is composed of two levels. The bottom level consists of the elementary circuitry, composed of *gates* and *flip-flops.* The upper level consists of a read-only memory *(ROM)* and a sequencing circuit. When a particular sequence is activated, the ROM produces a series of commands which causes the basic circuits to carry out some operation, such as adding the contents of two registers. Each sequence becomes an instruction in the upper level instruction set. Micro-programming is somewhat like a higher level language done in hardware. It makes the instruction set more concise, consistent, and powerful—and much easier to work with. By adding new sequences to the ROM, new instructions can be created. Or by changing the pattern in the ROM, the CPU can be made to look like a completely different machine, with a whole new instruction set. Most microprocessors are micro-programmed.

Microsecond. One millionth of a second.

Millisecond. One thousandth of a second.

Minicomputer. It used to be that a minicomputer was a computer with a word length of 18 *bits* or less, about 4 *K* of memory, a simplified instruction set, and available at a very low cost. Now that microprocessors are doing many of the things that minis used to do, minis are improving in performance and putting pressure on larger computers.

Mixed mode. Refers to the use of two different types of variable, such as integer and floating point, in the same expression. Some compilers will choke on this, while others will convert from one representation to the other automatically and proceed on that basis.

Mnemonic. A mnemonic is an abbreviated name for a computer instruction, such as "JMP," "ADD," or "CLR." The computer can be programmed to translate these into the 1's and 0's it understands. The mnemonic names are much easier to remember, which is what "mnemonic" means.

Modem. It is often convenient to communicate with a distant computer over a telephone line. However, computer pulses cannot be sent over an ordinary phone line. The modem converts the computer's pulses into beeps and chirps that can be sent over the phone line. The distant computer answers with its chirps and beeps, and your modem converts them back into pulses for your equipment.

Modular. Composed of sub-units. Both computer systems and programs are made this way to make them easier to change or expand.

Monitor. This is the program that coordinates the rest of the system. It loads whatever compiler is being called for, keeps track of input and output, bills your account number for the proper amount of time, and kills programs that run longer than they should. It may also be called a *supervisor, executive,* or *operating system.*

Monte Carlo method. This technique involves random sampling or models of events which depend on chance. It is named after the famous casino because it requires the use of random numbers. As an example, assume we want to measure the area of an irregular closed curve drawn on a piece of paper. Pick a random point on the paper and note whether it falls inside or outside the curve. If this process is repeated many times, the ratio of points falling inside the curve to points falling outside will begin to give us an idea of the area enclosed by the curve. The Monte Carlo method is not very efficient, often requiring thousands of trials to give useful results. The high speed of the computer is what makes its use possible.

MOS. Stands for Metal Oxide Semiconductor, an IC fabrication method which can produce very complex circuits at low cost.

MTBF. Stands for Mean Time Between Failures. An important indicator of reliability.

MTTR. Stands for Mean Time To Repair.

Multiplexing. Refers to the process of sending more than one signal over a single line.

Multiprocessing. In a multiprocessing system, two or more similar computers are hooked together. The individual computers can work on different parts of the same problem simultaneously, or on entirely different problems. Or each computer can specialize in a particular kind of task; or two computers can work on the same program and check each other.

Multi-programming. This is a mode of operation in which the computer divides its time among several programs, working on one for a while, then switching to another.

Naive user. Somebody who wants to use the computer to do something, but does not know much about computers or programming and does not particularly care to. Systems should always be designed with the naive user in mind. All of us are naive users at some time or other.

NAND. Short for NOT-AND, the logical negation of the AND function. A NAND B is false if both A and B are true; true otherwise.

NAND gate. This is an electronic circuit whose output is a "0" if all of its inputs are "1." It behaves like an *AND gate* hooked to an *inverter*.

Nanosecond. One billionth of a second.

Natural language. Refers to languages human beings are accustomed to speaking, such as English, French, German, etc. Their richness, ambiguity, and inconsistency make them very difficult for computers to understand, though a great deal of effort is being exerted in this direction. The ultimate dream of programmers is to be able to program in natural language. Some programming languages for specialized purposes approach this ideal.

Networks. Some computers are connected together by means of high-speed data links into networks. If one computer is overloaded, it can shift part of its burden to another. Network users can also exchange data and programs with one another.

Noise. Any variation in an electrical signal that is not supposed to be there. Causes include random electron motion, nearby electrical machinery, thunderstorms, maladjusted radio transmitters, and evil spirits. See *Glitch*.

Noise word. A nonessential word which is included in a program to improve readability, but which is ignored by the computer.

Non-destructive read. Used to describe a memory element which can be read from without destroying the information in it.

Non-maskable interrupt. Most *interrupt* lines can be disabled or "masked" by a program instruction so that all interrupts thereafter will be ignored by the computer. A non-maskable interrupt line, however, has first priority and can never be disabled. It is reserved for things which must not be ignored, such as the operator's console or a power failure alarm.

NOR. Short for NOT-OR, the logical negation of the OR function. A NOR B is false if either A or B is true; true otherwise.

NOR gate. This is an electronic circuit whose output is a "0" if any of its inputs is a "1." It behaves like an *OR gate* hooked to an *inverter*.

Nucleus. A basic collection of routines kept in main memory at all times.

Number crunching. Refers to long or complex calculations.

Numerical analysis. Deals with methods for finding useful solutions to problems once they have been stated mathematically. Numerical analysis also studies errors that arise during calculations and how they may be kept within limits.

Numerical control. Controlling a machine or process by means of digitally encoded numeric data is called "numerical control." The control information can be prerecorded, or the equipment can be under the direct control of a computer.

Nybble. A nybble is a piece of information half the length of a *byte,* or 4 bits long. Who says computer folk have no sense of humor?

Object module. An object module consists of an *object program* plus the control information the computer needs to load it and combine it with other object programs.

Object program. This is the machine language program that a compiler produces from the programmer's source program in high-level language. It's the one that the computer actually executes.

OCR. Stands for Optical Character Recognition. Documents can now be read by machine, using two special type faces that have been standardized for this purpose. This is faster, cheaper, and less error-prone than manual keyboard entry.

Octal. A number system which uses only 8 digits. Here are the numbers from 0 to 16 in decimal, octal, and binary:

Decimal	Octal	Binary
1	01	000001
2	02	000010
3	03	000011
4	04	000100
5	05	000101
6	06	000110
7	07	000111
8	10	001000
9	11	001001
10	12	001010
11	13	001011
12	14	001100
13	15	001101
14	16	001110
15	17	001111
16	20	010000

In octal, each place has eight times the value of the place to its left. At the right is the one's place, then the eight's place, then the sixty-four's place, and so on. So octal represents ten as one eight plus two or 12.

Now comes the reason for taking up octal in the first place. If we separate the bits of the binary numbers into groups of three and write for each group its decimal equivalent, we have an instant translation of binary into octal. This is very convenient, for long strings of bits are both cumbersome and hard to remember, while octal notation is much more compact and convenient. Wouldn't you rather remember 110001100110 as 6146?

Odd parity. See under *Parity.*

Off. Said of an electronic element that is not conducting current.

Offline. Not connected directly to the computer system.

Offset. This is a number which the computer adds to a *base address* to get a new *effective address.*

On. Said of an electronic element that is conducting current.

On line. Any equipment or process that sends information directly to the computer for immediate processing and immediate results is said to be on line. This is in contrast with storing the information and having the computer process it later.

On-line compiler. See *Incremental compiler.*

One-dimensional array. See *Array.*

Op code. Short for operation code. It's the part of a machine language instruction that tells the computer what it is to do next.

Operand. Something which is to be operated upon or manipulated. It may be a number, an address, a string, etc.

Operating system. A program which helps to overcome the

problems involved in running a computer. It makes sure that the proper programs are in the right place in memory at the right time, handles input and output operations, and allows the computer to work for long periods without the direct intervention of the operator. Also called *monitor, executive,* or *supervisor.*

Operation code. See *Op code.*

Operation cycle. This is the series of operations the CPU goes through. First it fetches the word containing its next instruction from memory, using the address in the program counter. The instruction is loaded into the instruction register and 1 is added to the program counter. The CPU decodes the instruction. If necessary, the CPU computes an effective address and places it in the address register. Finally the CPU executes the instruction and prepares to start the cycle over again.

Operator. An operator is a symbol which indicates an operation to be performed, such as + , − , *, etc.

Optical Character Recognition. See *OCR.*

OR. This is one of the computer's logical operations. It causes the computer to look at two words bit by bit. The result is a "1" if either the first bit *or* the second bit is a "1." For example, 11001010 OR 00011001 gives us 11011011.

OR gate. This is an electronic circuit whose output is a "1" if any of its inputs is "1."

Output. Information which results from the computer's manipulations and which is to be delivered to the outside world. Common output devices include line printers, teletypewriters, video terminals, card punches, paper tape punches, COM's and magnetic tape drives.

Overflow. When the result of some operation is too large for the computer to represent, an overflow occurs. Usually a light lights somewhere on the console when this happens.

Overhead. This is time that the computer spends keeping the system going, instead of working on somebody's program.

Overlay. If a program is too large to fit the computer's memory space, the parts that will not be needed immediately are stored externally and loaded into main memory as needed. These sections are called overlays.

Pack. To put several items in a single computer word.

Paging. Some computers have operating systems that chop a program up into segments called pages. Only the pages that are actually being used at a given moment need be kept in main memory. The rest can be on disk or tape. With paging, a program can be run that is larger than the computer's memory.

Paper tape punch. This device stores information on a strip of paper tape by punching holes in it. Each character is represented by a row of holes across the tape, plus a sprocket hole. Characters are usually entered by a keyboard. Teletype machines often have a paper tape punch.

Paper tape reader. This device senses the presence or absence of holes in punched paper tape, one character at a time, and produces electrical signals suitable for computer input.

Parallel. Refers to something that transmits or processes several bits at a time, as opposed to *serial* operation, in which bits are handled one by one. Parallel operation is typically faster than serial, but more expensive because several identical circuits are required in place of one.

Parameter. Parameters are data passed to a procedure or subroutine by the main program, or data produced by the procedure which it passes to the main program.

Parity. In order to detect errors, a single *bit* (called the parity bit) is often attached to computer words. The parity bit is chosen so that the total number of 1's in the word is either even (even parity) or odd (odd parity). The receiving equipment checks the number of bits in each word: if it is odd instead of even (or vice versa), a bit has been changed somewhere along the way and a light flashes saying "parity error." If two bits in a word are altered, the parity check is no help at all, but that doesn't happen very often (one hopes).

Parsing. The process of scanning a *string* to determine its components.

Partition sort. The partition sort divides a *file* into subsets, each of which may be sorted further. As an example, assume we have a long list of numbers. Pick an arbitrary number A from the list and put it at the top. Scan the list from the top down, looking for a number greater than A. When one is found, call it E. Now scan the list from the bottom up, looking for a number less than A. When one is found, call it F and swap E and F. Now go back to scanning down from the top. When the two scans meet in the middle of the list, the sort is done. Now swap A with the last E. The list is now in three parts: numbers less than A, A, and numbers greater than A. The partition sort is also called the "quicksort." For large numbers of elements, it is faster than the *bubble sort*.

Pass. Each time an assembler or compiler goes through a source program it completes one pass. Most assemblers make two passes; a compiler may make several.

Password. In multiple user systems, users are often asked to identify themselves with a password, unique to each user, before the computer will let them use the system.

Patch. A patch is a group of instructions that have been shoehorned into a program to correct an error or deficiency. Patching a program rather than rewriting it is poor practice, for a program with numerous patches becomes very hard to understand.

Peripheral. A peripheral is a device that is attached to a computer system but is not essential to its basic operation. Most peripherals are input or output devices of some sort, or devices for storing large amounts of data.

Pipelining. A "pipelined" microprocessor has an overlapping *operation cycle,* so that while it is executing the current instruction, it is getting ready for the next one. Pipelining increases the speed of microprocessors greatly.

PL/I. A programming language that grew out of a project to improve FORTRAN. PL/I is intended as a multipurpose language, capable of doing everything other languages can do and eventually replacing them. PL/I is very general, very powerful, and very complex.

Plotter. This device allows the computer to control a pen moving over a piece of paper and make pictures. Because the pen moves in two dimensions, it is sometimes called an X-Y plotter.

Pointer. A pointer is a number attached to a piece of information that tells the computer where to find some related piece of information.

Polish notation. Devised by Jan Lukasiewicz, this system of notation allows arithmetic expressions to be written and evaluated without parentheses. It's called Polish notation because few people can pronounce Lukasiewicz properly. In Polish notation A + B looks like + AB. The computer starts at the right and scans to the left. Each time it finds an operand, it puts it on a *stack*. When it finds an operation, it takes the top two items off the stack, performs the operation, and puts the result back on the stack. Finally there is just one number left in the stack, the answer. As an example we will evaluate $(5 + 7 - 2)/3$, which looks like $/ - + 5723$ in Polish:

stack	expression
empty	/ − + 5723_
3	/ − + 572<u>3</u>
3 2	/ − + 57<u>2</u>3
3 2 7	/ − + 5<u>7</u>23
3 2 7 5	/ − + <u>5</u>723
3 2 12	/ − <u>+</u> 5723
3 10	/ <u>−</u> + 5723
3.33	<u>/</u>− + 5723

There is also reverse Polish notation, in which the scan proceeds from left to right.

Polling. Sometimes several devices are connected to a single *interrupt* line. When an interrupt occurs, the computer has to interrogate or "poll" each device to find which one caused the interrupt.

Port. An *input* or *output* connection to the computer.

Portable. A program is portable if it can be easily run on several different computers.

Power supply. The electronic circuits of a computer are unable to use AC voltage from the wall socket directly. The power supply converts it to low-voltage DC. The output of a computer power supply is also tightly regulated to keep noise pulses and voltage variations from upsetting the computer's circuits.

Precedence of operations. In order to write expressions unambiguously, you must first know in what order the computer does its operations. Usually anything inside parentheses is evaluated first. Then comes exponentiations, then multiplication and division, then addition and subtraction. But it's best not to take anything for granted — when in doubt, use parentheses.

Precision. The number of digits in a number. Please notice it has nothing to do with accuracy!

Prettyprinting. Prettyprinting is the use of spaces and blank lines to make a program more readable. Statements controlled by another line are indented under it. This makes the logical structure of a program much clearer.

Primitive. The smallest and simplest elements of a programming language.

Printed Circuit. More properly "etched circuit." A thin layer of copper is bonded to an insulating board made of phenolic or fiberglass. When immersed in a chemical etching bath, the copper is dissolved away, except on those areas of the board that have been coated with a material that resists the action of the etchant. The copper left on the board forms the wiring of the circuit.

Printer. See *Line printer, Teletype*.

Privileged instruction. A computer instruction which is available only to the operating system or supervisory programs, and not the general user.

Problem-oriented language. A badly overused phrase. You are safe only in assuming that the language referred to will be easier to use in solving some problem than *assembly language*.

Problem-solving language. A language which can be used to specify a complete solution to a problem.

Procedure. Another name for a *subroutine*.

Procedure-oriented language. A programming language in which the operations to be performed are all executable and their sequence is specified by the user. This term applies to most familiar programming languages.

Processor status word. See *Status word*.

Program. The sequence of instructions designed to make the computer carry out a given task.

Program counter. The program counter is a special register in the computer. Each time the computer finishes an instruction, it adds 1 to the program counter, which then points to the location in memory of the next instruction.

Program listing. A complete copy of a program.

Programming. The task of writing a series of instructions that will cause the computer to do something useful. The first (and often the hardest) step is to define the problem as completely and in as much detail as possible. Next the programmer must devise a procedure for carrying out the task, being careful to check that his procedure will work properly in all conceivable circumstances. Only then should he start writing the instructions that form the actual program. The program is tested and revised, or rewritten if it doesn't work properly. When satisfied that the program works as intended, the programmer writes a description of how it works so that other programmers will be able to understand it and change or extend it if necessary.

Programming language. Synonymous with *high-level language*.

Pseudo code. Refers to a series of natural language statements arranged in a manner resembling a program. There is no firm connection with any actual programming language. Used for instructional purposes or as a preliminary "rough sketch" of a program. (See *Loop* for an example.)

Pseudo-op. The pseudo-op (or pseudo-operator) is a directive used in *assembly language* to control the operation of the assembler. The pseudo-op does not appear in the machine language program produced by the assembler. A typical pseudo-op is the word "END" written at the end of a program to tell the assembler its work is done.

Pseudorandom number. Random numbers are required for certain applications (such as the *Monte Carlo method*). One way of getting them is to put a table of random numbers in the computer's memory. This can take up too much valuable memory space, so it is usually better to have the computer generate its own random numbers. Since the computer must do this by following a sequence of fixed rules, such numbers are not truly random. Hence they are called pseudorandom numbers.

Publication language. A well-defined form of a programming language suitable for printing. A publication language is necessary because some languages use special characters which are not available in normal type.

Pulse. A sudden and abrupt jump in an electrical quantity from its usual level to a higher or lower value, quickly followed by an equally abrupt return.

Punched card. Few people have escaped an encounter with one of these slips of cardboard with the enigmatic little holes and its mystic injunction not to "fold, spindle, or multilate." Punched cards have been around a lot longer than computers. The standard card has 80 columns and 12 rows. A single punch in one of the first 10 rows is a number. An extra punch in one of the top three rows means a letter or symbol. Given a card out of the blue, it is not difficult to translate punches into symbols; but unless you know something about the program, what the symbols mean to the computer is anybody's guess.

Punched paper tape. This is a popular medium for storing information in small systems. The tape has seven or eight lengthwise rows of holes (also called channels), plus a row of sprocket holes for guiding it through reading mechanisms. Each crosswise row of holes represents a single character.

Pushdown list. An alternative name for a *stack*.

Queue. A queue is a data structure that in some ways

resembles a *stack*. In a stack items are added and removed only from one end, whereas in a queue items are added at one end and removed from the other. This resembles a queue waiting at a ticket window; hence the name.

Quicksort. See under *Partition sort*.

Radix. The radix (or base, or root) of a number system is the number of digits that can appear in it. The radix of the *decimal* system is ten, of *binary* two, of *octal* eight, of *hexadecimal* sixteen, and so on. In its own system, the radix is always written as 10.

RAM. Short for Random Access Memory.

Random access. You can write or read information from a random access memory element any time you like, instead of waiting for it to come around to the right position, as with a tape, disk, or drum. Same as direct access.

Reader check. If a card reader finds an invalid character on a card it is reading, it stops at once so the offending card can be removed.

Read-only memory. See *ROM*.

Read/write head. See *Head*.

Real numbers. Some computer languages use the word "real" to mean a number in *floating point* form, though integers are real numbers too from the viewpoint of mathematics.

Real-time. A real-time system is one that can keep up with events in the outside world. A computer in an air traffic control system must be real-time, for instance, since it can hardly take an hour or two to think about what to do if two planes are approaching each other on collision courses.

Real-time clock. A device that signals the computer at regular intervals so it can keep up with some event in the outside world.

Record. A record is a collection of information consisting of one or more related items. (See also *Block*.)

Recursive. A statement or process is recursive if it calls its own self into operation as a part of its workings. Here is a recursive definition: a multiple of ten is ten *or* any multiple of ten multiplied by ten.

The definition tells us 10 is a multiple of ten; so is 10 x 10 or 100. 100 is a multiple of 10, so 100 x 10 or 1000 is a multiple of 10 too. And so on. In spite of the fact that the multiples of ten are infinite, this definition accounts for them all simply and concisely. Programs can be written recursively too. It is a very powerful technique.

Re-entrant. A re-entrant program or *subroutine* is written in such a way that it can be used by many users concurrently. The alternative is to let each user have his own copy of the program, which uses up a lot of memory space. A re-entrant program cannot be allowed to modify its own instructions.

Reference language. The definitive description of a programming language, completely specifying all its concepts and the relations between them. It may be in English, a specialized notation, or the language itself may be the reference language.

Register. A register is a special kind of memory location built into the CPU. Most computers have several. This is where the computer does things to information. The contents of registers can be added, shifted, compared, complemented, swapped, and so on. Or a register can just be used to store data temporarily. The CPU can get information in and out of the registers much faster than it can from main memory, so programmers try to use the registers as much as possible.

Relational operators. These are the symbols for "equal to"

(=); "not equal to" (≠); "greater than" (>); "less than" (<); "greater than or equal to" (≥); "less than or equal to" (≤). They are usually used in *conditional statements,* such as: IF A ≥ B, GO TO 47.

Relative addressing. An addressing mode in which the computer is told to look so many locations ahead or behind the current instruction to find the desired memory location.

Relocating loader. It often happens that it is desirable to put a program into a section of memory different from the one for which it was originally written. A relocating loader takes the program, plus relocation inf⸱rmation, makes appropriate adjustments to all the addresses, and loads the program in its new location.

Remote. Refers to equipment located at a distance. A large computer is often shared by many users who communicate with it over telephone lines or other data links.

Reset. One *resets* a flag, flip-flop, or bit by making it "0".

Resident. Present in the system or in memory.

Response time. This is the time it takes for the user of a time-sharing system to get back an answer to what he just typed.

Restart. An error during the course of a long program usually means the whole thing must be done over again — an expensive waste of time. To avoid this, the computer is asked periodically to store its intermediate results. If an error occurs, the computer is taken back to its last set of correct results and continues on from there in what is called a restart.

Ring. A ring is a special kind of linked list, in which we have a string of items and the last item points back to the first item. Also called a *circularly-linked list* or a *cycle*.

Roll in, roll out. If a computer must shift its mode of operation quickly, it can store the contents of its memory on disk (roll out) and read in a complete new program (roll in).

ROM. Short for Read Only Memory. Information once planted in it cannot be erased or destroyed. ROM's are handy for holding things like tables and subroutines that are used frequently.

Rotate. A computer instruction that causes the *bits* in a word to be shifted a certain number of places left or right. The bits that get "pushed off the end" reappear at the other end of the word. For instance, 10110111 rotated three places to the right is 11110110.

Round-off error. If the computer produces more digits in a result than can be used, it is far better to round off rather than to just throw away the unwanted digits (*truncation*). The error is usually too small to worry about. But if the computer uses the rounded-off result for further calculations and the process is repeated many times, the error can become severe and the programmer has to take it into account.

RS-232. This is the most widely used standard for serial data transmission. Devices that are RS-232 compatible can be connected together with a minimum of fuss.

Scientific notation. When writing very large numbers like 186,000,000, it becomes bothersome to have to write so many zeroes. 186,000,000 is the same as 1.86 times 100,000,000; and 100,000,000 can be written as 10^8 (10 times itself 8 times). So we can write that number as 1.86×10^8 and save a lot of time. The 10^8 tells us to move the decimal point 8 places to the right if we want the full number with all the zeroes. We can write very small numbers the same way. The number .000047 comes out as 4.7×10^{-5}. The 10^{-5} tells us to move the decimal point 5 places to the left. Very large and very small numbers occur all the time in scientific work; hence the term scientific notation. Computers use this idea too, but there it's called *floating point*.

Scratch pad memory. This is a small very fast memory that the computer can use in which to store data temporarily. This makes operations faster than they would be if the computer had to use the slower but less expensive main memory for everything.

Search. The process of finidng a particular item in a *file*. Search techniques include the *sequential* or linear search, the *binary* or logarithmic search, and *direct lookup*.

Second generation. Refers to the computers using transistors in place of vacuum tubes, which began to appear in the middle 1950's.

Sector. For purposes of addressing information, the surface of a magnetic disk is considered to be divided up into a series of wedge-shaped segments called sectors.

Security. Designers of multi-user systems have two difficult problems; how to keep unauthorized people from using the system, and how to keep users from reading or changing each other's files.

Seek time. This is the time it takes a disk drive to move its heads from one track to another

Selection sort. The selection sort is a simple sorting *algorithm* for putting all the elements in a *file* in order. As an example, assume we are sorting a list of numbers. Go down the list looking for the smallest number. When you find it, swap it with the first number in the list. Now repeat the search process, starting with the second number on the list (since the first number is already the smallest). When the smallest number is found, exchange it with the second number in the list. Begin the search again, starting with the third number on the list. The search and swap process continues until all the numbers in the list are placed in ascending order. The selection sort is good for small files, but not too efficient for very large ones.

Sense switches. These are switches on the front panel or console of the computer. You can program the computer to check a switch and take some action depending on whether it is on or off.

Sequential access. Refers to memories in which the computer cannot refer to the particular location it wants immediately, but must wait until it comes along. Examples are magnetic disks, drums, and tapes.

Sequential search. This is the simplest possible search and the least efficient. The computer looks at items one by one until it finds the one it is looking for. Also called "linear search."

Serial. Refers to something that transmits or processes a series of bits one at a time, as opposed to *parallel* operation, in which several bits are handled at once.

Set. One *sets* a flag, flip-flop, or bit by making it "1".

Setup time. Refers to time spent by the computer operator in changing tapes, loading cards into the card reader, setting switches, and otherwise preparing for the next program.

Shift. A computer instruction that causes the bits in a word to be shifted right or left a certain number of places. The bits that "drop off the end" are lost. The empty space at the other end is filled with zeros. For instance, if 10110111 is shifted right three places, we have 00010110.

Sifting. Refers to translation by the computer from one *high-level language* to another similar language.

Sign bit. The leftmost *bit* of a computer word is sometimes used to indicate whether the number it contains is positive or negative. Usually a zero means a positive number, and a "1" a negative number.

Simplex. A simplex data line is one that transmits data in only one direction.

Simulation. Through simulation, a computer may be used to imitate the behavior of a process or system. The thing to be simulated is represented by a mathematical model set up in the computer. By changing conditions in the model, experiments can be performed that would be too difficult, expensive, or dangerous to try in real life. For instance, engineers can "construct" a bridge, try different variations, even subject their design to a phantom hurricane, all without touching a single rivet.

Snapshot. A printout of intermediate results partway through the program run. A very handy *debugging* aid.

SNOBOL. SNOBOL is a programming language which grew out of linguistics research. It is a *string* processing language, good at things like pattern matching and text analysis.

Software. The word software refers to a computer's programs. If a particular bit of data manipulation is done through a program rather than by special circuitry, it is said to be "in software." Doing things in software is cheap and flexible, since a program can be easily changed; but it takes time.

Software maintenance. Improvements and changes are always being made in software. Bugs turn up even in long established programs. The task of keeping software up to date and working properly is called software maintenance.

Sort. A procedure designed to arrange a group of elements in random order into some kind of a sequence. Examples include the *bubble sort,* the *selection sort,* and the *partition sort.*

Source document. A paper containing information that is to be read into the computer.

Source program. This is the program that the programmer writes in *high-level language.* It must be turned into machine language before it can be run on the computer.

Special purpose language. A programming language which is designed to satisfy a single specific objective.

Spooling. This term comes from the acronym SPOOL, which stands for Simultaneous Peripheral Output On Line. Spooling now refers to the computer's ability to control I/0 processes at the same time it is doing its regular work. This keeps the computer from having to wait for the slow I/0 devices.

Stack. The stack is a region of memory which works by special rules. Each time the computer stores a word there, it goes "on top of the stack," and all the previously stored words move down one level. When a computer takes a word off the top of the stack, everything moves up one level, until the stack is empty. Noice the computer has access only to the top of the stack. Piling a word on the stack is called a "push," and taking a word off is called a "pull" or a "pop." The stack simplifies some operations enormously.

Stand-alone. Refers to a system or piece of equipment that is capable of doing its job without being connected to anything else.

State. A description of the internal condition of a machine, indicating what it has done recently and what it is about to do next.

Status word. The status word (or processor status word), together with the contents of the registers, defines the computer's state or condition at any given moment. If the computer is interruped, it must save the status word so it can return to its former task.

Stochastic. Random.

Storage. See *Memory*.

Stored program concept. This idea, due to Von Neumann, is the most important single idea associated with computers.

Instead of being wired to do a specific job, the computer uses instructions stored in a *memory*. By changing these instructions, the behavior of the computer is changed, making the computer the closest thing to a true general-purpose machine yet devised by man. The same memory is used to store both instructions and data. The sequence "11000001" may mean the letter "A" or it may mean "clear the accumulator." The computer cannot tell which is what except in the context of its instructions. This gives the computer the ability to manipulate instructions as though they were data.

String. A string is a line of symbols of indefinite length treated as a single unit. This is the way the computer sees text. It is possible to talk about "character strings," "text strings," "alphanumeric strings," "string manipulation," and so on.

Structured programming. Structured programming (also called top-down programming) is a systematic procedure for writing programs in modular form with a clear logical structure. Such programs are easy to understand and modify.

First the programmer defines the problem as exactly as he can, with samples of the desired input and output if possible. Next, he writes an outline procedure for solving the problem. It resembles a program, but the statements in it are much broader and more general than those available in any programming language, and they are in ordinary English. At this point, the programmer is thinking about the problem, not about any specific language or machine. The programmer now checks his "program" to make sure that it produces the correct results.

Next, the programmer refines his procedure, making it more detailed. He considers alternatives and backtracks if necessary. He checks the new version to verify its correctness. This process of successive refinement is continued until the procedure is broken down to a point where it may be written in an existing programming language. Notice that fine details are put off until they become relevant. *Subroutines* are written to fit the structure of the main program rather than the other way round. Most important, at any point in the process, the programmer has a "program" whose correctness can be verified.

Subroutine. When a task must be repeated many times in the course of a program, it is usually taken out and made into a small sub-program which can be called up by the main program as needed. This is a subroutine.

Subscripted variable. A subscripted variable is one that has one or more numbers attached to it, indicating its place in a series or *array*.

Successive approximation. This is a technique often used in the solution of equations by computer. The computer (or the user) makes a guess at the solution. The guess is put into the equation and the result is used to make another guess which is closer to the true solution. The process is repeated, getting closer each time, until a sufficiently accurate solution is obtained.

Supervisor. A program that helps manage the operation of a computer system. (See *Operating systems.)*

Swap. Refers to the process of moving part of a program from main memory to external storage (tape or disk) so that another piece of program can be moved from external storage to main memory. Swapping reduces computer efficiency, but it allows the system to get along with less memory.

Symbolic address. It is very convenient to refer to memory locations by the names of their contents instead of having to remember the numbers of actual address locations. This is symbolic addressing. The computer takes the names you give it, matches them up with appropriate address locations, and keeps all the bookkeeping straight.

Symbolic logic. See *Boolean algebra.*

Synchronous. Most computers are designed so that each operation proceeds one step upon receiving a pulse from a master source or *clock*. Everything that goes on is synchronized by the clock pulses. The computer isn't quite as fast as it would be if everything went at its own speed, but the problem of controlling all the various sections is much simplified.

Syntax. Every computer language has rules about how its commands may be used and how they fit together. These rules make up its syntax.

System. A collection of devices that work together to accomplish some meaningful result.

Systems program. A systems program controls the operations of the computer system, in contrast with an *applications program,* which is intended to solve a problem or to do a job.

Systems software. This consists of all the programs that tie together and coordinate the devices that make up the computer system. It includes such programs as loaders, compilers, interpreters, and input/output routines.

Tape drive. Most large computer installations have several of these for reading and storing information on magnetic tape. They are easy to spot by the large tape spools moving jerkily on their fronts.

Teletype®. The Teletype is a popular computer terminal. It looks like a large typewriter. The Teletype is noisy and slow and its numerous moving parts need regular maintenance. Its great advantage is that it provides a printed record of all that passes between the user and the computer. The most commonly used model, the 33ASR, includes a paper tape reader and punch.

Terminal. A terminal is a device for communicating with the computer. It usually consists of a keyboard plus either a video screen (video terminal) or a printing mechanism like a typewriter (Teletype).

Text editor. A text editor is a program that allows you to manipulate text by adding words, deleting words, transposing sentences, and so on. The text being worked on is usually a program, but it could just as well be a love letter or the next chapter of your novel.

Think time. This is the time the user of a *time-sharing* system spends just sitting at his terminal, not using the computer.

Thrashing. It always seems that a program segment has been swapped out of main memory just before it is needed, making it necessary to swap it back in. This is called "thrashing."

Throughput. Refers to the total volume of work performed by a computer in a given period of time.

Tie-breaker. Refers to circuitry that resolves the conflict when two CPU's try to use the same device at once.

Time-sharing. Time-sharing was developed to overcome the disadvantages of *batch* processing. It enables many people to use the computer at once. Each user sits before a terminal which he uses to type in his program or make changes in it. The computer does a small part of one user's program, then quickly shifts to the next user. The computer can do this so quickly that each user has the feeling of being alone with the computer. The biggest advantage of time-sharing is immediate response from the computer, and a chance to change your program right away if it didn't work right the first time.

Time-slicing. This is a type of operation in which the computer works on one program for a short time, then goes to another program and works on that for a short time, and so forth.

Top-down programming. Another name for *structured programming*.

Trace. This is a *debugging* aid which gives the programmer a record of the contents of the program counter and the main registers after each instruction is executed. Should be used with discretion, otherwise it will overwhelm you with paper.

Track. Information is recorded on the surface of a magnetic disk in a series of concentric circles. Each of these is called a track.

Transparent. Refers to something the equipment does that the user is not aware of. He "sees right through it."

Trap. A trap occurs when the computer senses an unusual condition, such as an overflow. Program execution stops, a message is printed out, and the program is usually terminated.

Tree. A tree is a special kind of linked *list.* Each item points to several items below it, and each of these points to several items below *it,* and so on. The whole thing looks like the roots of a tree.

Tri-state® . Refers to a circuit that is specially constructed so that it can be signalled to isolate itself from whatever is connected to its output.

Truncation. If there are too many digits in a number for the computer to represent it properly, the extra digits are simply chopped off and thrown away. This operation, called truncation, can lead to serious errors unless the programmer knows what he is doing. Computers generally do not round off unless they are programmed to. See also *Round-off error.*

T²L. See *TTL.*

TTL. TTL (sometimes written T²L) stands for Transistor-Transistor Logic, a family of digital logic IC's presently in widespread use.

TTY. A common abbreviation for *Teletype.*

Turing machine. The Turing machine, conceived by A.M. Turing, is the most primitive computer it is possible to imagine. Its program and data are on an infinitely long paper tape which it can advance or rewind one step at a time. It can detect the presence or absence of a mark on the tape, and it can erase a mark or make a mark of its own. The Turing machine is capable, in principle, of doing anything any computer can do. While it would be rather pointless to build one, the Turing machine is a very useful theoretical concept, for it is helpful in proving theorems about what tasks computers can or cannot do.

Turing test. The Turing test is a famous concept in the field of *artificial intelligence.* How do you decide when a computer can be called intelligent? The Turing test provides a practical answer. You sit down at a terminal and converse with whoever is at the other end of the line. Your terminal might be connected to the computer or to another terminal with a human being seated behind it (you don't know which). If after a while you can't decide whether you've been talking to a human being or to the computer, the computer may be said to be intelligent for all practical purposes. (Some conversational programs have been written which appear to pass the Turing test, but these are merely collections of programming tricks and do not show true intelligence.)

Turn-around time. This is the time it takes to get your results back after you submit a program. It may range from seconds, if you are sitting at a time-sharing terminal, to days, if your program is being run as part of a low-priority batch.

Two-dimensional array. See *Array.*

Two's complement. It is possible to handle subtraction in binary just as you learned it in school, with borrowing and so on. To distinguish negative numbers from positive ones, we can make the leftmost bit in the computer word a *sign bit,* making it 0 for a negative number and 1 for a negative one. This gives us signed binary numbers.

But it happens that there is an easier way to subtract in binary. Most modern computers use *two's complement* notation. This is a way of representing negative numbers that allows the computer to subtract by adding. To complement a binary number, just turn all the 1's into 0's and all the 0's into 1's. To get the two's complement, add 1. Examples:

00010110	22	00001100	12
11101001	complemented	11110011	complemented
+1	plus 1	+1	plus 1
11101010	2's complement	11110100	2's complement
	−22		−12

Notice that in this scheme, negative numbers end up with their leftmost bit a 1. To subtract a number from another, we put it into two's complement form and add. As an example, let's see how a computer with an 8-bit word length would subtract 12 from 26:

00011010	26
+11110100	−12
100001110	14

We get the expected answer, 1110 or fourteen, except that a ninth bit has popped up on the left as a carry. However, there is no room for this bit in our 8-bit word, so it would simply be lost, leaving us with the correct answer, 00001110. If we had subtracted 26 from 12, we would have gotten a negative 14, in two's complement notation. No matter what combination of positive and negative numbers is involved, the leftmost bit always gives the sign correctly, and any negative answers appear in two's complement form. Try it.

UART. Short for Universal Asynchronous Receiver/Transmitter. This is an integrated circuit that is finding increasing use in data handling equipment. One half of it converts *parallel* data into *serial* form; the other half performs the reverse operation.

Underflow. An underflow occurs when the result of some operation is too small for the computer to represent. The value may be very significant; but to the computer, it is zero.

Unpack. To separate items previously combined in a single computer word.

Up and running. Said of a computer system or piece of equipment that has just been put into operation and is working properly.

Upward compatible. If a piece of equipment can do everything the previous model could, plus a little more, it is said to be "upward compatible." Salesmen are very fond of this phrase.

User-oriented. Set up for somebody who is not expected to be knowlegeable about computers.

Utility program. A program made available by the operating system to save programmers the bother of writing their own programs to do often needed tasks.

Variable. A variable is an area in *memory* to which you have given a name. Usually you expect to put data there which you will manipulate in some fashion. The term variable comes from algebra.

Vector. A vector is a one-dimensional *array;* that is, a row of numbers each of which is assigned a subscript in serial order. The word vector is also sometimes used as a synonym for "pointer."

Video graphic display. Computers can do more with video screens than display words on them. They can be made to draw pictures too, using dots or lines. They can rotate objects, show them in perspective, move them around, stretch or shrink them. Such things as color and 3-D presentation are possible too. Computer movies have been made. This sort of capability is expensive and limited mostly to one-of-a-kind systems at research centers now, but it is so exciting we can expect to see a lot more of it in the future.

Video terminal. The video terminal has a keyboard for sending information to the computer and a picture tube like a TV set's for displaying information. The video terminal is fast, silent, and has no moving parts. Its chief drawback is that it does not make a permanent record of the information displayed.

Virtual memory. Short for virtually unlimited memory. See *paging.*

Volatile. Used to describe a memory whose information vanishes when the power is turned off. A computer's registers are volatile, while magnetic core memories are not.

Von Neumann machine. This is the classic computer architecture, with an arithmetic/logic unit to perform operations, a memory unit to store instructions and data, an input unit, an output unit, and a control unit which interprets instructions and give commands to the other units.

Wait state. This is a condition in which the CPU is idle, not executing instruction. However, *interrupts* can occur.

Wire wrap®. A way of making electrical connections without soldering. A special tool wraps the wire tightly around a square post. The sharp edges bite into the wire, producing a reliable connection.

Word. Most computers can handle only a fixed number of bits at a time. This group of bits is called a word. The longer the word, the larger the numbers it can represent, or the greater the range of instructions it can express. Larger business and scientific computers usually have words 32 or more bits long, while minicomputers typically have 12- or 16-bit word lengths. Microprocessors usually have an 8-bit word length. A few computers have a variable word length.

Wrap-around. A computer word is something like a car milometer in that when it is holding the largest number it can hold, adding 1 causes it to go to zero. This means that the computer's address space does not end with the highest address, but "wraps around" to the beginning.

Zero suppression. In order to make results more readable, it is a good idea to delete leading zeroes from numbers. For instance, 00000682 becomes 682.

Appendix

Key to ASCII Code

NUL	Null Idle	DC1	Device Control 1
SOH	Start of Heading	DC2	Device Control 2
STX	Start of Text	DC3	Device Control 3
ETX	End of Text	DC4	Device Control 4 (Stop)
EOT	End of Transmission	NAK	Negative Acknowledge
ENQ	Enquiry	SYN	Synchronous Idle
ACK	Acknowledge	ETB	End of Transmission
BEL	Bell (audible signal)		Block
BS	Backspace	CAN	Cancel
HT	Horizontal Tab	EM	End of Medium
	(or punched card skip)	SUB	Substitute
LF	Line Feed	ESC	Escape
VT	Vertical Tab	FS	File Separator
FF	Form Feed	GS	Group Separator
CR	Carriage Return	RS	Record Separator
SO	Shift Out	US	Unit Separator
SI	Shift In	ƀ	blank
DLE	Data Link Escape	DEL	Delete

To find the code for a particular letter or symbol, take the first three bits from the column, and the remaining four bits from the row. For instance, "A" is 1000001. An eighth, or parity bit, is often added to make the total number of 1's in the group either odd or even for error detection purposes. The special codes with the abbreviated names are for controlling terminals or peripheral devices.

USA Standard Code for Information Interchange (ASCII)

b_7	0	0	0	0	1	1	1	1
b_6	0	0	1	1	0	0	1	1
b_5	0	1	0	1	0	1	0	1
$b_4 b_3 b_2 b_1$								
0 0 0 0	NUL	DLE	ḅ	0	@	P	`	p
0 0 0 1	SOH	DC1	!	1	A	Q	a	q
0 0 1 0	STX	DC2	"	2	B	R	b	r
0 0 1 1	ETX	DC3	#	3	C	S	c	s
0 1 0 0	EOT	DC4	$	4	D	T	d	t
0 1 0 1	ENQ	NAK	%	5	E	U	e	u
0 1 1 0	ACK	SYN	&	6	F	V	f	v
0 1 1 1	BEL	ETB	'	7	G	W	g	w
1 0 0 0	BS	CAN	(	8	H	X	h	x
1 0 0 1	HT	EM	)	9	I	Y	i	y
1 0 1 0	LF	SUB	*	:	J	Z	j	z
1 0 1 1	VT	ESC	+	;	K	[	k	{
1 1 0 0	FF	FS	,	<	L	\	l	¦
1 1 0 1	CR	GS	—	=	M	]	m	}
1 1 1 0	SO	RS	·	>	N	↑	n	~
1 1 1 1	SI	US	/	?	O	←	o	DEL

Logic Gate Symbols

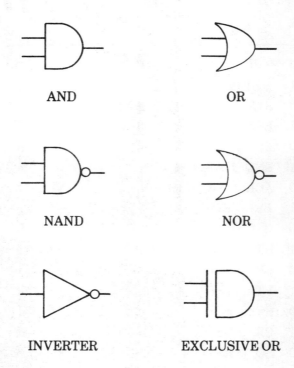

AND

OR

NAND

NOR

INVERTER

EXCLUSIVE OR

Note the small circle that is drawn on the output of some gates to indicate negation or inversion of the logic function.

Star

The Language

OF

ASTROLOGY

If you can't tell a conjunction from a configuration, a mean motion from a matutine, or primary directions from points of illumination, THE LANGUAGE OF ASTROLOGY can save you hours of valuable time.

Star

The Language OF ACCOUNTANCY

If you can't tell a balance sheet from a bond fund, a cost centre from a clearing house, or simple interest from subordinated debt — you could save yourself valuable time and money by learning THE LANGUAGE OF ACCOUNTANCY.

Star

The Language

OF

MARTIAL ARTS

If you don't know aikido from ashi-tori, the cat stance from the crab's claw, or an immovable elbow from inner power — you could save yourself from painful mispronunciation and injury by learning THE LANGUAGE OF MARTIAL ARTS.

The Language OF PHOTOGRAPHY

If you don't know your hot-shoe from your hardener, your shutter release from your SLR, or your safelight from your self-timer — THE LANGUAGE OF PHOTOGRAPHY can save you valuable time and money.

Star

The Language
OF
SAILING

If you don't know your stays from your kicking strap, your bungs from your batons, or whether you're heading up or bearing away – THE LANGUAGE OF SAILING can save you from a sea of troubles.